KEEP
CALM

YOU'RE ONLY

50

summersdale

KEEP CALM YOU'RE ONLY 50

An Hachette UK Company
www.hachette.co.uk

Summersdale Publishers Ltd
Part of Octopus Publishing Group Limited
Carmelite House
50 Victoria Embankment
LONDON
EC4Y 0DZ
UK

www.summersdale.com

Printed and bound in China

ISBN: 978-1-78783-307-4

Substantial discounts on bulk quantities of Summersdale books are available to corporations, professional associations and other organisations. For details contact general enquiries: telephone: +44 (0) 1243 771107 or email: enquiries@summersdale.com.

TO ....

FROM ....

THE KEY TO
SUCCESSFUL AGEING
IS TO PAY AS LITTLE
ATTENTION TO IT
AS POSSIBLE.

JUDITH REGAN

THE THREE
AGES OF MAN:
YOUTH, MIDDLE AGE AND "MY
WORD, YOU DO LOOK WELL".

JUNE WHITFIELD

IT TAKES A LONG TIME TO BECOME YOUNG.

PABLO PICASSO

BY THE TIME WE
HIT 50... WE HAVE
LEARNED TO TAKE
LIFE SERIOUSLY, BUT
NEVER OURSELVES.

MARIE DRESSLER

HAPPY 20TH ANNIVERSARY
OF YOUR 30TH BIRTHDAY!

ANONYMOUS

I'm happy to report
that my inner child
is still ageless.

JAMES BROUGHTON

TO ME, OLD AGE IS
ALWAYS 15 YEARS
OLDER THAN I AM.

BERNARD BARUCH

IF YOU HAVEN'T
GROWN UP BY AGE 50,
YOU DON'T HAVE TO.

ANONYMOUS

ABOUT THE ONLY THING THAT COMES TO US WITHOUT EFFORT IS OLD AGE.

GLORIA PITZER

AS A GRADUATE OF
THE ZSA ZSA GABOR
SCHOOL OF CREATIVE
MATHEMATICS, I
HONESTLY DO NOT
KNOW HOW OLD I AM.

ERMA BOMBECK

Forty is the old age of youth; Fifty the youth of old age.

VICTOR HUGO

I'D LIKE TO GROW VERY OLD
AS SLOWLY AS POSSIBLE.

CHARLES LAMB

HOW OLD WOULD YOU
BE IF YOU DIDN'T KNOW
HOW OLD YOU WERE?

SATCHEL PAIGE

THE WOMAN WHO

TELLS HER AGE IS EITHER TOO
YOUNG TO HAVE ANYTHING
TO LOSE OR TOO OLD TO HAVE
ANYTHING TO GAIN.

CHINESE PROVERB

FEW WOMEN ADMIT THEIR AGE. FEW MEN ACT THEIRS.

ANONYMOUS

I REFUSE TO ADMIT
I'M MORE THAN 52,
EVEN IF THAT DOES
MAKE MY SONS
ILLEGITIMATE.

NANCY ASTOR

NO WOMAN SHOULD
EVER BE QUITE ACCURATE
ABOUT HER AGE. IT LOOKS
SO CALCULATING.

OSCAR WILDE

In dog years,
I'm dead.

ANONYMOUS

FOR ALL THE
ADVANCES IN
MEDICINE, THERE
IS STILL NO CURE
FOR THE COMMON
BIRTHDAY.

JOHN GLENN

BIRTHDAYS ONLY
COME ONCE A YEAR UNLESS
YOU'RE JOAN COLLINS, IN
WHICH CASE THEY ONLY
COME EVERY FOUR YEARS.

STEVE BAUER

I INTEND TO LIVE FOREVER, OR DIE TRYING.

GROUCHO MARX

WHEN YOU'RE 50 AND
WAKE UP WITHOUT
ANY ACHES AND PAINS,
YOU KNOW IT'S GOING
TO BE A GOOD DAY.

MELANIE WHITE

To keep the heart unwrinkled, to be hopeful, kindly, cheerful, reverent – that is to triumph over old age.

THOMAS BAILEY ALDRICH

A HUG IS THE PERFECT
GIFT; ONE SIZE FITS ALL,
AND NOBODY MINDS IF
YOU EXCHANGE IT.

ANONYMOUS

YOUTH IS WHEN
YOU'RE ALLOWED
TO STAY UP LATE ON
NEW YEAR'S EVE.
MIDDLE AGE IS WHEN
YOU'RE FORCED TO.

BILL VAUGHAN

A GIFT,

WITH A KIND
COUNTENANCE, IS
A DOUBLE PRESENT.

THOMAS FULLER

AT MY AGE, FLOWERS SCARE ME.

GEORGE BURNS

AGE IS JUST A
NUMBER. IT'S TOTALLY
IRRELEVANT UNLESS,
OF COURSE, YOU
HAPPEN TO BE A
BOTTLE OF WINE.

JOAN COLLINS

YOUTH IS THE GIFT OF
NATURE, BUT AGE IS
A WORK OF ART.

GARSON KANIN

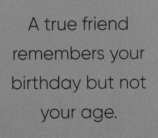

A true friend remembers your birthday but not your age.

ANONYMOUS

HANDMADE PRESENTS
ARE SCARY BECAUSE
THEY REVEAL THAT
YOU HAVE TOO
MUCH FREE TIME.

DOUGLAS COUPLAND

TIME IS THE COIN

OF YOUR LIFE. IT IS THE ONLY
COIN YOU HAVE, AND ONLY
YOU CAN DETERMINE HOW IT
WILL BE SPENT. BE CAREFUL
LEST YOU LET OTHER PEOPLE
SPEND IT FOR YOU.

CARL SANDBURG

THE OLD AGE OF AN EAGLE IS BETTER THAN THE YOUTH OF A SPARROW.

PROVERB

YOU'RE NOT FIFTY – YOU'RE FIVE PERFECT TENS!

ANONYMOUS

Birthdays are good for you. Statistics show that the people who have the most live the longest.

LARRY LORENZONI

WHENEVER THE TALK
TURNS TO AGE, I SAY
I AM 49 PLUS VAT.

LIONEL BLAIR

WE KNOW WE'RE
GETTING OLD WHEN
THE ONLY THING
WE WANT FOR OUR
BIRTHDAY IS NOT TO
BE REMINDED OF IT.

ANONYMOUS

AGE IS NOT IMPORTANT,

UNLESS YOU'RE A CHEESE.

HELEN HAYES

THE YEARS
TEACH MUCH
WHICH THE DAYS
NEVER KNOW.

RALPH WALDO EMERSON

EVERY TIME I THINK
THAT I'M GETTING
OLD, AND GRADUALLY
GOING TO THE
GRAVE, SOMETHING
ELSE HAPPENS.

ELVIS PRESLEY

GROWING OLD IS
MANDATORY; GROWING
UP IS OPTIONAL.

CHILI DAVIS

Ageing is not "lost youth" but a new stage of opportunity and strength.

BETTY FRIEDAN

ONE OF THE BEST
PARTS OF GROWING
OLDER? YOU CAN
FLIRT ALL YOU
LIKE SINCE YOU'VE
BECOME HARMLESS.

LIZ SMITH

ANOTHER BELIEF
OF MINE: THAT EVERYONE ELSE
MY AGE IS AN ADULT, WHEREAS
I AM MERELY IN DISGUISE.

MARGARET ATWOOD

THE LONGER I LIVE, THE MORE BEAUTIFUL LIFE BECOMES.

FRANK LLOYD WRIGHT

ONE OF THE MANY
THINGS NOBODY EVER
TELLS YOU ABOUT
MIDDLE AGE IS THAT IT'S
SUCH A NICE CHANGE
FROM BEING YOUNG.

DOROTHY CANFIELD FISHER

If you find yourself 50 years old and you aren't doing what you love, then what's the point?

JIM CARREY

NICE TO BE HERE?
AT MY AGE, IT'S NICE
TO BE ANYWHERE.

GEORGE BURNS

IT IS A MISTAKE TO
REGARD AGE AS A
DOWNHILL GRADE
TOWARD DISSOLUTION.
THE REVERSE IS TRUE.
AS ONE GROWS OLDER,
ONE CLIMBS WITH
SURPRISING STRIDES.

GEORGE SAND

ZEAL, N.

A CERTAIN NERVOUS
DISORDER AFFLICTING THE
YOUNG AND INEXPERIENCED.

AMBROSE BIERCE

AT MY AGE "GETTING LUCKY" MEANS FINDING MY CAR IN THE PARKING LOT.

ANONYMOUS

I BELIEVE IN LOYALTY: I THINK WHEN A WOMAN REACHES A CERTAIN AGE SHE LIKES SHE SHOULD STICK TO IT.

EVA GABOR

OLD PEOPLE AREN'T
EXEMPT FROM HAVING
FUN AND DANCING...
AND PLAYING.

LIZ SMITH

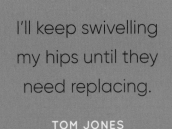

I'll keep swivelling
my hips until they
need replacing.

TOM JONES

IT'S SEX, NOT
YOUTH, THAT'S
WASTED ON
THE YOUNG.

JANET HARRIS

MIDDLE AGE IS
HAVING A CHOICE BETWEEN
TWO TEMPTATIONS AND
CHOOSING THE ONE THAT'LL
GET YOU HOME EARLIER.

DAN BENNETT

THE YOUNG SOW WILD OATS. THE OLD GROW SAGE.

WINSTON CHURCHILL

YOU KNOW YOU'RE
KNOCKING ON WHEN
YOU FEEL LIKE THE-
MORNING-AFTER-THE-
NIGHT-BEFORE WITHOUT
HAVING BEEN ANYWHERE.

ANONYMOUS

A man is a fool if he drinks
before he reaches 50,
and a fool if he doesn't
drink afterward.

FRANK LLOYD WRIGHT

THE AGEING PROCESS HAS
YOU FIRMLY IN ITS GRASP IF
YOU NEVER GET THE URGE
TO THROW A SNOWBALL.

DOUG LARSON

I'M LIMITLESS AS FAR
AS AGE IS CONCERNED...
AS LONG AS HE HAS A
DRIVER'S LICENCE.

**KIM CATTRALL ON
DATING YOUNGER MEN**

THERE'S A KIND OF
CONFIDENCE THAT COMES
WHEN YOU'RE IN YOUR FORTIES
AND FIFTIES, AND MEN FIND
THAT INCREDIBLY ATTRACTIVE.

PEGGY NORTHROP

OLD WOOD BEST TO BURN, OLD WINE TO DRINK, OLD FRIENDS TO TRUST, AND OLD AUTHORS TO READ.

FRANCIS BACON

WE'VE BOTH HIT 50,
AND WE CELEBRATE IT.
THERE IS NO DOOMY
SIDE TO IT... WE'RE
NEARLY GROWN-UP
NOW, BUT NOT QUITE.

DAWN FRENCH AND
JENNIFER SAUNDERS

WE ARE ALWAYS THE
SAME AGE INSIDE.

GERTRUDE STEIN

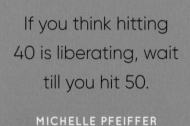

If you think hitting
40 is liberating, wait
till you hit 50.

MICHELLE PFEIFFER

YOU CAN'T TURN
BACK THE CLOCK
BUT YOU CAN WIND
IT UP AGAIN.

BONNIE PRUDDEN

I DON'T BELIEVE IN
AGEING. I BELIEVE IN FOREVER
ALTERING ONE'S ASPECT TO
THE SUN. HENCE MY OPTIMISM.

VIRGINIA WOOLF

I'M AIMING BY THE TIME I'M 50 TO STOP BEING AN ADOLESCENT.

WENDY COPE

THE OLD BELIEVE
EVERYTHING; THE
MIDDLE-AGED SUSPECT
EVERYTHING; THE YOUNG
KNOW EVERYTHING.

OSCAR WILDE

I'm surprised that I'm 50...
I still feel like a kid.

BRUCE WILLIS

A YOUNG MAN IS
EMBARRASSED TO
QUESTION AN OLDER ONE.

HOMER

CHILDREN ARE A GREAT
COMFORT IN YOUR
OLD AGE – AND THEY
HELP YOU REACH
IT FASTER, TOO.

LIONEL KAUFFMAN

WHEN GRACE

IS JOINED WITH WRINKLES,
IT IS ADORABLE. THERE IS AN
UNSPEAKABLE DAWN IN
HAPPY OLD AGE.

VICTOR HUGO

GROWING OLD IS A BAD HABIT WHICH A BUSY MAN HAS NO TIME TO FORM.

ANDRÉ MAUROIS

MY MOTHER IS
GOING TO HAVE TO
STOP LYING ABOUT
HER AGE BECAUSE
PRETTY SOON I'M
GOING TO BE OLDER
THAN SHE IS.

R. TRIPP EVANS

AS IS A TALE, SO IS LIFE:
NOT HOW LONG IT IS,
BUT HOW GOOD IT IS,
IS WHAT MATTERS.

SENECA

A man is not old
as long as he is
seeking something.

JEAN ROSTAND

WITH AGE COMES THE INNER, THE HIGHER LIFE. WHO WOULD BE FOREVER YOUNG, TO DWELL ALWAYS IN EXTERNALS?

ELIZABETH CADY STANTON

TO WIN BACK

MY YOUTH... THERE IS
NOTHING I WOULDN'T DO –
EXCEPT TAKE EXERCISE, GET
UP EARLY OR BE A USEFUL
MEMBER OF THE COMMUNITY.

OSCAR WILDE

THE MORE YOU COMPLAIN, THE LONGER GOD LETS YOU LIVE!

ANONYMOUS

THE GREAT THING
ABOUT GETTING OLDER
IS THAT YOU DON'T
LOSE ALL THE OTHER
AGES YOU'VE BEEN.

MADELEINE L'ENGLE

A friend never defends a husband who gets his wife an electric skillet for her birthday.

ERMA BOMBECK

I ABSOLUTELY REFUSE
TO REVEAL MY AGE.
WHAT AM I – A CAR?

CYNDI LAUPER

YOUNG MEN'S MINDS ARE
ALWAYS CHANGEABLE,
BUT WHEN AN OLD MAN
IS CONCERNED IN A
MATTER, HE LOOKS BOTH
BEFORE AND AFTER.

HOMER

FROM 40 TO 50

A MAN MUST MOVE UPWARD,
OR THE NATURAL FALLING
OFF IN THE VIGOUR OF
LIFE WILL CARRY HIM
RAPIDLY DOWNWARD.

OLIVER WENDELL HOLMES JR

NONE ARE SO OLD AS THOSE WHO HAVE OUTLIVED ENTHUSIASM.

HENRY DAVID THOREAU

THE BEST WAY TO
GET MOST HUSBANDS
TO DO SOMETHING
IS TO SUGGEST THAT
PERHAPS THEY'RE
TOO OLD TO DO IT.

ANNE BANCROFT

YOU ARE ONLY YOUNG
ONCE, BUT YOU CAN BE
IMMATURE FOR A LIFETIME.

JOHN P. GRIER

Old age puts more
wrinkles in our minds
than on our faces.

MICHEL DE MONTAIGNE

ONE OF THE SIGNS
OF PASSING YOUTH
IS THE BIRTH OF A
SENSE OF FELLOWSHIP
WITH OTHER HUMAN
BEINGS AS WE
TAKE OUR PLACE
AMONG THEM.

VIRGINIA WOOLF

THE OLD BEGIN

TO COMPLAIN OF THE
CONDUCT OF THE YOUNG
WHEN THEY THEMSELVES ARE
NO LONGER ABLE TO SET
A BAD EXAMPLE.

FRANÇOIS DE LA ROCHEFOUCAULD

TO KNOW HOW TO GROW OLD IS THE MASTERWORK OF WISDOM.

HENRI-FRÉDÉRIC AMIEL

I HAVE ENJOYED
GREATLY THE SECOND
BLOOMING... SUDDENLY
YOU FIND – AT THE AGE
OF 50, SAY – THAT A
WHOLE NEW LIFE HAS
OPENED BEFORE YOU.

AGATHA CHRISTIE

He's so old that when he
orders a three-minute
egg, they ask for the
money up front.

MILTON BERLE

THE SURPRISING THING
ABOUT YOUNG FOOLS IS
HOW MANY SURVIVE TO
BECOME OLD FOOLS.

DOUG LARSON

BECOMING A
GRANDMOTHER IS
WONDERFUL. ONE
MOMENT YOU'RE JUST
A MOTHER. THE NEXT
YOU ARE ALL-WISE
AND PREHISTORIC.

PAM BROWN

BEFORE YOU CONTRADICT

AN OLD MAN, MY FAIR
FRIEND, YOU SHOULD
ENDEAVOUR TO
UNDERSTAND HIM.

GEORGE SANTAYANA

NO MAN IS EVER OLD ENOUGH TO KNOW BETTER.

HOLBROOK JACKSON

WRINKLES SHOULD
MERELY INDICATE
WHERE SMILES
HAVE BEEN.

MARK TWAIN

AGE MERELY SHOWS WHAT CHILDREN WE REMAIN.

JOHANN WOLFGANG VON GOETHE

He who laughs, lasts!

MARY PETTIBONE POOLE

TOMORROW'S GONE — WE'LL HAVE TONIGHT!

DOROTHY PARKER

NO MATTER
HOW OLD YOU ARE, THERE'S
ALWAYS SOMETHING GOOD
TO LOOK FORWARD TO.

LYNN JOHNSTON

TO STOP AGEING, KEEP ON RAGING.

MICHAEL FORBES

THE OTHER DAY A
MAN ASKED ME WHAT I
THOUGHT WAS THE BEST
TIME OF LIFE. "WHY," I
ANSWERED... "NOW."

DAVID GRAYSON

Just remember, once you're over the hill you begin to pick up speed.

CHARLES M. SCHULZ

MIDDLE AGE IS WHEN
WE CAN DO JUST AS
MUCH AS EVER — BUT
WOULD RATHER NOT.

ANONYMOUS

THE FOLLIES WHICH A
MAN REGRETS MOST
IN HIS LIFE ARE THOSE
WHICH HE DIDN'T
COMMIT WHEN HE HAD
THE OPPORTUNITY.

HELEN ROWLAND

ONE CAN REMAIN

ALIVE LONG PAST THE USUAL
DATE OF DISINTEGRATION IF
ONE IS UNAFRAID OF CHANGE,
INSATIABLE IN INTELLECTUAL
CURIOSITY, INTERESTED IN
BIG THINGS AND HAPPY
IN SMALL WAYS.

EDITH WHARTON

THE TIME TO BEGIN MOST THINGS IS TEN YEARS AGO.

MIGNON McLAUGHLIN

NOBODY GROWS
OLD MERELY BY
LIVING A NUMBER
OF YEARS. WE GROW
OLD BY DESERTING
OUR IDEALS.

SAMUEL ULLMAN

NO MAN LOVES LIFE LIKE
HIM THAT'S GROWING OLD.

SOPHOCLES

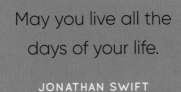

May you live all the
days of your life.

JONATHAN SWIFT

YOU CAN LIVE TO BE
A HUNDRED IF YOU
GIVE UP ALL THE
THINGS THAT MAKE
YOU WANT TO LIVE
TO BE A HUNDRED.

ANONYMOUS

THE AVERAGE CHILD

LAUGHS ABOUT 400 TIMES
PER DAY; THE AVERAGE ADULT
LAUGHS ONLY 15 TIMES PER
DAY. WHAT HAPPENED TO
THE OTHER 385 LAUGHS?
LAUGH AND LIVE!

ANONYMOUS

THE PURPOSE OF LIFE IS TO FIGHT MATURITY.

DICK WERTHIMER

AGE DOES NOT
PROTECT YOU
FROM LOVE. BUT
LOVE, TO SOME
EXTENT, PROTECTS
YOU FROM AGE.

JEANNE MOREAU

The only reason I would take up jogging is so that I could hear heavy breathing again.

ERMA BOMBECK

TIME DOTH FLIT;
OH SH*T!

DOROTHY PARKER

YOU KNOW YOU'VE
REACHED MIDDLE
AGE WHEN YOUR
WEIGHTLIFTING
CONSISTS MERELY
OF STANDING UP.

BOB HOPE

MY DOCTOR

TOLD ME TO DO
SOMETHING THAT PUTS
ME OUT OF BREATH, SO I'VE
TAKEN UP SMOKING AGAIN.

JO BRAND

MIDDLE AGE IS WHEN YOU CHOOSE YOUR CEREAL FOR THE FIBRE, NOT THE TOY.

ANONYMOUS

THE YEARS BETWEEN 50 AND 70 ARE THE HARDEST. YOU ARE ALWAYS BEING ASKED TO DO THINGS, AND YOU ARE NOT YET DECREPIT ENOUGH TO TURN THEM DOWN.

T. S. ELIOT

DO NOT WORRY ABOUT
AVOIDING TEMPTATION.
AS YOU GROW OLDER
IT WILL AVOID YOU.

JOEY ADAMS

Old age is no
place for sissies.

BETTE DAVIS

I FEEL STRONGER
NOW THAN, MAYBE,
20 YEARS AGO.
IF YOUR MIND IS
STRONG, YOUR BODY
WILL BE STRONG.

MADONNA

MIDDLE AGE

IS THE TIME WHEN A MAN IS
ALWAYS THINKING THAT IN A
WEEK OR TWO HE WILL FEEL
AS GOOD AS EVER.

DON MARQUIS

IF I'D KNOWN I WAS GOING TO LIVE THIS LONG, I'D HAVE TAKEN BETTER CARE OF MYSELF.

EUBIE BLAKE

I NEVER WORRY
ABOUT DIETS. THE ONLY
CARROTS THAT INTEREST
ME ARE THE NUMBER
YOU GET IN A DIAMOND.

MAE WEST

I don't feel old. I don't feel anything till noon. That's when it's time for my nap.

BOB HOPE

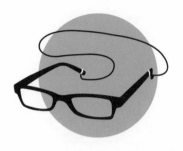

THE ONLY FORM OF EXERCISE
I TAKE IS MASSAGE.

TRUMAN CAPOTE

OLD MINDS ARE LIKE
OLD HORSES; YOU MUST
EXERCISE THEM IF YOU
WISH TO KEEP THEM
IN WORKING ORDER.

JOHN ADAMS

AGE SELDOM
ARRIVES SMOOTHLY OR
QUICKLY. IT'S MORE OFTEN
A SUCCESSION OF JERKS.

JEAN RHYS

PEOPLE WHO SAY YOU'RE JUST AS OLD AS YOU FEEL ARE ALL WRONG, FORTUNATELY.

RUSSELL BAKER

WHAT MOST PERSONS
CONSIDER AS VIRTUE,
AFTER THE AGE OF
40 IS SIMPLY A
LOSS OF ENERGY.

VOLTAIRE

LIFE IS EITHER A DARING
ADVENTURE OR NOTHING.

HELEN KELLER

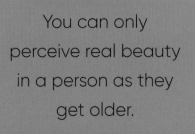

You can only
perceive real beauty
in a person as they
get older.

ANOUK AIMÉE

MIDDLE AGE IS WHEN
YOUR AGE STARTS
TO SHOW AROUND
YOUR MIDDLE.

BOB HOPE

YOU KNOW YOU'RE

GETTING OLD WHEN YOU
STOP TO TIE YOUR SHOES AND
WONDER WHAT ELSE YOU
CAN DO WHILE YOU'RE
DOWN THERE.

GEORGE BURNS

GREY HAIR IS
GOD'S GRAFFITI.

ANONYMOUS

THE AGE OF A
WOMAN DOESN'T
MEAN A THING.
THE BEST TUNES
ARE PLAYED ON THE
OLDEST FIDDLES.

RALPH WALDO EMERSON

I don't plan to grow old gracefully; I plan to have facelifts until my ears meet.

RITA RUDNER

REGRETS ARE THE NATURAL
PROPERTY OF GREY HAIRS.

CHARLES DICKENS

I WAS GETTING
DRESSED AND A PEEPING
TOM LOOKED IN THE
WINDOW... AND PULLED
DOWN THE SHADE.

JOAN RIVERS

PLEASE DON'T

RETOUCH MY WRINKLES.

IT TOOK ME SO LONG

TO EARN THEM.

ANNA MAGNANI

WHEN IT COMES TO STAYING YOUNG, A MIND-LIFT BEATS A FACELIFT ANY DAY.

MARTY BUCELLA

THERE IS ONLY ONE
CURE FOR GREY HAIR.
IT WAS INVENTED
BY A FRENCHMAN.
IT IS CALLED THE
GUILLOTINE.

P. G. WODEHOUSE

I'M LIKE OLD WINE.
THEY DON'T BRING ME
OUT VERY OFTEN, BUT
I'M WELL PRESERVED.

ROSE KENNEDY

I'm not denying my age; I'm embellishing my youth.

TAMARA REYNOLDS

MIDDLE AGE IS
YOUTH WITHOUT
LEVITY, AND AGE
WITHOUT DECAY.

DANIEL DEFOE

NATURE GIVES YOU
THE FACE YOU HAVE AT 20, BUT
IT'S UP TO YOU TO MERIT THE
FACE YOU HAVE AT 50.

COCO CHANEL

SHE WAS A HANDSOME
WOMAN OF 45 **AND
WOULD REMAIN SO
FOR MANY YEARS.**

ANITA BROOKNER

THE SECRET OF
STAYING YOUNG IS
TO LIVE HONESTLY,
EAT SLOWLY AND LIE
ABOUT YOUR AGE.

LUCILLE BALL

AGE IS A NECESSARY
BUT INSUFFICIENT
REQUIREMENT FOR
GROWING UP.

HENRY CLOUD

KEEP
CALM

YOU'RE ONLY

50

If you're interested in finding out more about our books, find us on Facebook at **Summersdale Publishers** and follow us on Twitter at **@Summersdale**.

www.summersdale.com